NATIONAL GEOGRAPHIC

Living Traditions

PIONEER EDITION

By Cristina G. Mittermeier, Jennifer Peters, and Cheryl Block

CONTENTS

Painted People

BY CRISTINA G. MITTERMEIER

Meet the people of Papua New Guinea.

Huli Hunters. *Huli men carry spears, bows, and arrows to hunt and to protect their families.*

I fought to stay awake in the afternoon heat. I was on a boat with friends. We floated up a river in Papua New Guinea. It is a nation in the Pacific Ocean.

My boat headed toward a village. We looked for people. But we didn't see them. We docked. I grabbed my camera. Then I jumped out of the boat. Suddenly, painted faces surrounded me. The **indigenous people** greeted me. Indigenous people are related to the first people in a place.

I am a photographer. I take pictures of people all over the world. Still, I love Papua New Guinea best. I love taking pictures of this beautiful country and its amazing people.

Tribal Life

More than 1,000 groups of people live in Papua New Guinea. Some do not get along with their neighbors. Cliffs and jungles keep some groups apart. That keeps them from fighting.

Each group has a different culture. A culture is a way of life. It includes language, food, and more.

I love to learn about each culture. It helps me understand people.

Take the Huli, for example. Men and women live apart, even when they are married. Men hunt and wear colorful wigs. Women do most of the work. They raise kids. They grow sweet potatoes. They care for pigs. They support their **community**.

Works of Art

Spirit houses are some of the most important buildings. They are sacred places. They are places where people worship gods. Almost every group has a spirit house. In many groups, only men can go inside the spirit houses.

I am a woman. But I paid to go inside a spirit house. I did not know what I would see. The inside of the spirit house stunned me. It was filled with beautiful objects. There were shields, statues, and large hooks. Each one had been carefully painted. They were all amazing works of art.

What Did You Say?

There are 850 languages spoken in Papua New Guinea. People speak more languages here than anywhere else. I tried to communicate with people there. I tried even though I didn't speak their language. At times, I didn't know what they were saying to me. This could be confusing.

Most of the time, I communicated well, however. I tried to show people how I see things. Usually, I was able to understand, too. That's important. I want to understand how other people see the world. That helps me understand my own world better.

Sacred Art. *These paintings decorate the inside of a spirit house.*

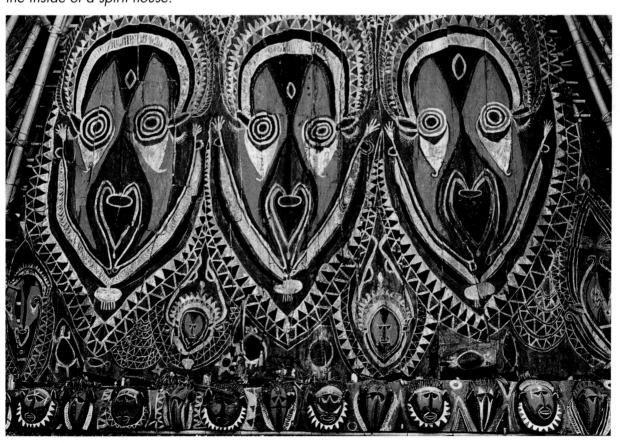

Colorful Dance. *These dancers show off their costumes. They are at a festival on Mount Hagen.*

Fabulous Festivals

At the end of my trip, I went to Mount Hagen. It is a tall mountain. Many groups were having a **festival** there. The people were having a big party.

More than 40,000 people went to the festival. They celebrated their past. They wore colorful costumes. They danced, told stories, and had fun.

I walked with my camera. Drums thundered. Feathers swayed. Feet stomped. I saw people in great hats.

I even saw some mud men. They wore amazing masks made of mud.

Plenty of Photos

I started taking photos. There was so much happening. Soon a line formed near me. Painted people wanted me to take their pictures. I went through 100 rolls of film. I could not stop. The people were so beautiful.

The sun rose higher in the sky. The light was too bright to take pictures. I put my camera away. I walked into the crowd of painted people.

I took in all the sounds, smells, and colors of the day. Being surrounded by these strangers scared me a little.

Yet their smiles made me forget that I was far from home. We were all together, having fun. We were all part of the same wonderful world.

Mud Men. *These men wear masks made of mud. Their long claws are made of wood.*

HULI HAIR

BY JENNIFER PETERS

Caring for Hair. *Huli men wear mushroom-shaped wigs every day.*

Imagine that your future depended on perfect hair. For Huli boys, it does. The Huli believe that hair shows strength. Men wear wigs to earn respect. They make wigs from their own hair. So nothing is as important as growing great hair.

A HIDDEN PEOPLE

The Huli live in Papua New Guinea. No one from the outside world knew about them until the 1930s. Today, there are about 70,000 Huli people. Most choose to follow their traditional way of life.

Where in the world is Papua New Guinea?

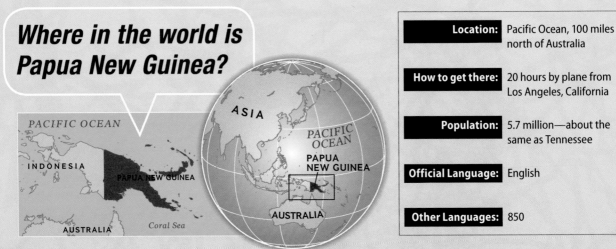

Location:	Pacific Ocean, 100 miles north of Australia
How to get there:	20 hours by plane from Los Angeles, California
Population:	5.7 million—about the same as Tennessee
Official Language:	English
Other Languages:	850

TRADITIONS AND RULES

As teenagers, many girls garden and babysit. Many boys go to wig school. There, boys learn the rules. 1) Don't run. That makes your hair bounce. 2) Stay away from fires. They could burn your hair. 3) Water your hair 12 times a day. That makes it grow faster. This way, boys learn to grow their hair for wigs. It is an important tradition.

BECOMING A MAN

A Huli male wears his first wig as a teen. It shows that he is ready for adulthood. He can wage war. He can even marry. To prepare, a boy grows his hair for months. Then he cuts it. A wigmaker makes the hair into wig. Boys add style with flowers and feathers. Later, they'll grow more wigs. The wigs show they are adults.

Festival Face. *A young boy wears face paint for a special occasion.*

Huli Hello. *A Huli man introduces tourists to his culture.*

How would your life be different... if you were a Huli?

	LUNCH	HOBBIES	CHORES	FOR FUN
Kids in the U.S.	P B & J sandwich	Play soccer	Clean room	Play video games
Huli boys	Frogs and mice	Collect flowers and feathers for wig	Water hair	Play bamboo flute
Huli girls	Sweet potatoes	Weave string bags	Work in garden	Shop at out-door market

Saving the World's Voices

By Cheryl Block

Scientists estimate that the world loses one language every 14 days. National Geographic's Enduring Voices Project works to preserve endangered languages around the world. They do this by finding language "hotspots." These include places where languages are in danger of dying out.

Why is language so important? Many ancient people shared traditions by speaking. They did not write down these traditions. Once we lose the speakers of these languages, we lose important knowledge of their cultures.

For example, some Australian cultures are at least 50,000 years old. In some cases, there are only one or two speakers of these cultures' languages. Scientists use technology to record the speakers. This helps preserve the languages. It also preserves the people's knowledge of the world.

NORTHWEST PACIFIC PLATEAU

OKLAHOMA-SOUTHWEST

MESOAMERICA

NORTHERN SOUTH AMERICA

CENTRAL SOUTH AMERICA

SOUTHERN SOUTH AMERICA

The Yupik people in the Arctic have almost 100 words for kinds of sea ice. Scientists could learn a lot about the Arctic from them.

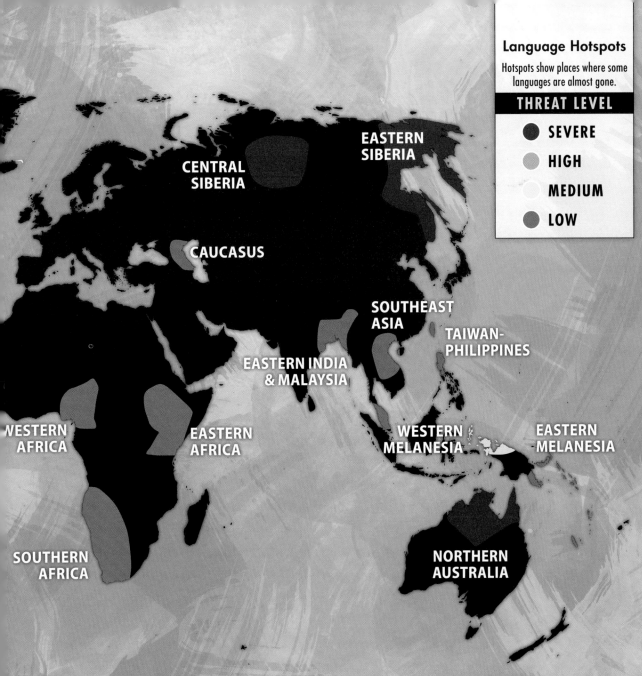

CENTRAL
SIBERIA

EASTERN
SIBERIA

CAUCASUS

SOUTHEAST
ASIA

TAIWAN-
PHILIPPINES

EASTERN INDIA
& MALAYSIA

WESTERN
AFRICA

EASTERN
AFRICA

WESTERN
MELANESIA

EASTERN
MELANESIA

SOUTHERN
AFRICA

NORTHERN
AUSTRALIA

Language Hotspots

Hotspots show places where some languages are almost gone.

THREAT LEVEL

- SEVERE
- HIGH
- MEDIUM
- LOW

Families of the Kallawaya people in Bolivia use a secret language to share what they know about plants.

Minyak	English
ནམ་སྟོན་པོ	blue sky
ཉི་མ	sun

Scientists in Tibet created a written form of the Minyak language. Elders wrote a textbook in Minyak and gave it to local schools.

Scientists recently discovered a hidden language in India. It is called Koro. It is spoken by only 800–1,200 people. They live with a group who speak a different languge.

CULTURAL CONNECTIONS

Connect to other cultures. Then answer the questions below.

1 Cristina Mittermeier does not speak the languages of Papua New Guinea. Why does she still try to talk to the people who live there?

2 Huli women support their community. What does *community* mean?

3 Huli boys wear wigs for the first time when they are teenagers. Why is this an important tradition?

4 The Enduring Voices Project works to preserve the world's languages. Why is this important?

5 Is language important for understanding other cultures? Why or why not?